The Work Ethic of Tom Brady,
Peyton Manning, and Aaron Rodgers

How Elite Athletes Prepare, Practice, and Think

Leadership Case Studies

Table of Contents

Introduction

Between 2001 and 2015, there have been a total of 15 Super Bowls played in the NFL.

10 of those Super Bowls had either Tom Brady, Aaron Rodgers, or Peyton Manning as a starting quarterback.

Between 2007 and 2015, there have been 8 winners of the NFL MVP award.

All but one were awarded to one of these three quarterbacks.

Throughout the past 15 years, these three quarterbacks have been widely considered to be the best at their positions. All three have won multiple league MVP awards, and all have led their teams to championships.

In a highly competitive industry where new players enter the league each year, how do these elite quarterbacks constantly play at a high level? All NFL coaches spend hours studying film and preparing their defenses to stop these quarterbacks. Yet, these three quarterbacks are able to lead their teams to victory each year.

In this leadership case study, we analyze the training mindset of these quarterbacks. It is said that being an NFL quarterback is one of the toughest positions to play in all of professional sports. So how do Brady, Rodgers, and Manning prepare for their jobs? How much time and effort do they put into training before the game?

The lessons from this case study can be applied to any person looking to improve their own performance. Whether you are an athlete, a working professional, or just looking to improve your performance, the training and practice tips of these elite quarterbacks can help you.

Please be aware that this is not a football book. We do not discuss how you can throw a tighter spiral, or how to read blitz coverages like Tom Brady. Rather, this case study focuses on the work ethic and mindset of the three quarterbacks.

In Chapter 1 of the case study, we focus on how the three quarterbacks PREPARE for their opponents. We discuss how much time and effort they put into studying football, how they schedule their time, and how there is a direct link between the time they study and their success on the field.

Chapter 2 focuses on how they view PRACTICE. We share quotes and stories about how these Pro Bowl quarterbacks treat practice. We discuss how they have specific goals that they want to accomplish during practice, and mention how Aaron Rodgers was able to use his time in practice to become one the best quarterbacks in the NFL.

The case study concludes in Chapter 3 with a focus on the MINDSET of the quarterbacks. Both Brady and Rodgers started their professional careers on the bench. We highlight how they didn't let the evaluations of others discourage them, but rather used it to as motivation. We focus on how they accomplished that, and how Brady learned to focus on the task at hand.

To help apply the lesson to your own performance goals, we have included a few review questions after each chapter.

All information in this case study has been collected from public sources. Links to the original articles and additional source information are available at our website, leadershipcasestudies.com.

Background Information

Tom Brady

Date of Birth: August 3, 1977

College: University of Michigan

Selected by the New England Patriots as the 199th pick of the 2000 NFL Draft.

4x Super Bowl Champion (2002, 2004, 2005, 2015)

3x Super Bowl MVP (2002, 2004, 2015)

2x NFL MVP (2007, 2010)

10x Pro Bowl Selections

Peyton Manning

Date of Birth: March 24, 1976

College: University of Tennessee

Selected by the Indianapolis Colts with the 1st pick of the 1998 NFL Draft.

Super Bowl Champion (2007)

Super Bowl MVP (2007)

5x NFL MVP (2003, 2004, 2008, 2009, 2012)

14x Pro Bowl Selection

Aaron Rodgers

Date of Birth: December 2, 1983

College: Butte Community College, University of California, Berkeley.

Selected by the Green Bay Packers with the 24th pick of the 2005 NFL Draft.

Super Bowl Champion (2011)

Super Bowl MVP (2011)

2x NFL MVP (2011, 2014)

4x Pro Bowl Selection

Preparation

Everyone works hard. That's a given. In any industry, everyone understands that hard work and long hours are needed to reach the top. The elite quarterbacks of the NFL are a great example of this. To fully understand how much work is needed to be the best in the world, a close examination of the study Tom Brady, Aaron Rodgers, and Peyton Manning is needed.

The first common trait of all three quarterbacks is that they all do individual work on their own time. They pay attention during team meetings, work hard during training sessions, and practice at a high intensity. But to them, the time put in during the work day is simply not enough. They each put in additional hours studying and preparing aside from what the normal team schedule.

For example, the Green Bay Packers have team meetings from 7:30 am to 10:00, practice on the field in the late morning, and then additional meetings in the afternoon. Quarterback Aaron Rodgers goes through these team activities, but then fires up his laptop at night to study on his own.

As Lori Nickel of the Milwaukee Journal Sentinel writes, "We see the stats." We see the arm strength of Rodgers, and the touchdowns and Lambeau leap. But we don't see the late night hours that Rodgers spends studying opposing defenses.

"What almost no one sees is Green Bay Packers quarterback Aaron Rodgers on Monday night. And Tuesday night. And every other night during the week," Nickel writes. "That's when he's on his own time, with the laptop computer, studying everything about the defense and looking at his own play with a critical eye." As former backup quarterback Matt Flynn said, Rodgers "does a lot on his own."

Peyton Manning has been putting in the extra hours since he was in high school. During Super Bowl 48, when Peyton Manning's Broncos were about to face the Seattle Seahawks, Rapper Lil Wayne gave an interesting story about the Manning brothers to the MMQB's Peter King.

According to Lil Wayne, one of his roadies was an ex con who was sent to a work release program in New Orleans. One of the roadies jobs was to be a school janitor at a local high school. Lil Wayne tells Peter King that because of the roadies role as a ex-con on a work release program, "he would have to clean the schoolyard at 4 or 5 in the morning. There was not one morning, 4:30, 5 in the morning, he wouldn't see Archie, Peyton, Cooper, or Eli out on the field. He'd see Archie throwing passes to Cooper, or Peyton throwing routes to Cooper."

"He (the roadie) would tell us the story, you know, like it was destined".
Elizabeth Merrill of ESPN also writes that Peyton's thorough preparation as a leader goes all the way back to his high school career.

"Here's how seriously Manning takes his role as leader: After his senior season of high school, when the team picked captains for the following year, Manning took the captains out to eat at Domilise's, his favorite po-boy restaurant in town. Manning spent the next hour explaining to the teenagers, in great detail, the importance of being in charge of a team."

Before he was even drafted by the Indianapolis Colts, Peyton Manning was already putting in the time and effort to succeed. When first meeting the team at the scouting combine, Manning demonstrated to the team that he was already studying and looking to find ways to become a great quarterback.

"He showed up for his 1988 interview at the scouting combine with the Colts - held in the city that would come to be his own - carrying a legal pad with a page and a half of questions," writes Les Carpenter of Yahoo Sports. "After the Indianapolis staff barraged him with inquiries, he pulled out the legal pad and interrogated them right back."

Tom Brady is also one to put in work early in the morning. Along with head coach Bill Belichick, Brady puts in the extra time to study the opposing defense for any advantage, as well to make sure that he is at peak physical form. Greg Bishop of Sports Illustrated writes about how former safety Rodney Harrison showed up at the Patriots facility at 6:40 am to lift weights. Tom Brady was already there, and he greeted Harrison with a "Good afternoon."

"So the next day Harrison showed up at 6:30. "Good afternoon." Then 6:20. Then 6:10. Then 6. "Good afternoon" each time, until Harrison finally said, "Screw you Tom. I'm not coming in any earlier", writes Bishop.

In fact, even after winning his fourth Super Bowl title, Tom Brady is still willing to put in the extra hours. According to the Collective Bargaining Agreement, there are certain restrictions for the amount of contact that a player can have with the team during the off-season. April 6, 2015 was the first day that the Patriots players were allowed back in the facility to meet with coaches. According to local media reports, Tom Brady was the first player in the building at exactly 7 am that day for the start of the Patriots offseason program.

Brady has also structured his entire life around maximizing his football potential. According to Bishop, Brady and his personal trainer have already written down what type of workout, treatment, and recovery Brady is to undertake for the next THREE YEARS. Every single day is mapped out, with what type of workouts to undertake, what type of foods to eat, and when to sleep.

Brady's trainer tells Bishop about a typical day for Brady during the offseason. "Brady wakes up, works out, has breakfast with Gisele and their two kids, hangs at the beach, naps on schedule, surfs, works out again. He goes to sleep early, eats well and for the most part avoids alcohol. The in-season portion of his regimen is designed to run through Super Bowl Sunday; if New England's campaign ends in a playoff loss, Brady completes every drill, every throw, anyway."

Here are just a few things that Brady does to make sure that his body and mind are functioning at a high level:

- He takes naps at specific times in order to rest his body and mind.
- He has a specific diet for the summer (mostly raw foods), and for the winter (red meat).
- He eats certain types of foods to "maintain balance and harmony through my metabolic system" such as hummus and raw snack bars. Or, as one teammate called it, "birdseed sh..".
- He undertook a brain scan in order to create a brain exercise program designed to help keep his sharp. He trained his brain to be able to process information faster, which helped him read defenses faster. It helped him increase his memory and increase his peripheral vision. It also is designed to help him in the event of a concussion.
- To help him unwind after games, he does a routine of cognitive exercises at night to help settle and relax his mind. This helps him fall asleep by 9 pm and allows him to get up
  - in the morning without an alarm.

What exactly they do:

Now that's it's clear that elite quarterbacks put in a lot of hours to honing their skills, what exactly are they doing during that time? It's one thing to say "work hard", or "you have to put in the time and effort to succeed." But what exactly does that mean? What are Aaron Rodgers, Peyton Manning, and Tom Brady actually doing during those long hours? How exactly are they studying?

1. Repetition

The number one thing that these three great quarterback do is familiarize themselves with the defense of their opponents. They are looking at film of the defense to see how they line up. They are remembering what the linebacker is doing when he lines up in a certain package. They are trying to find any spaces that open up when a certain type of coverage is deployed.

Basically, what they are doing is familiarizing themselves with their opponents. They are getting familiar with the situations that they will encounter on Sunday. They are getting comfortable with the situation so that when they see it during a game, there will be a sense of familiarity with it.

In essence, they are taking reps.

Think about any physical activity that a person learns. From hitting a curveball to learning how to serve a tennis ball, the more reps a person takes gives them the practice to learn the activity. If you can't hit a curveball, the more times you have a curveball pitched to you, then the better your chances of learning how to hit it.

This concept of repeatedly seeing situations can apply to areas outside of sports. In graduate business school courses, students are repeatedly taught "Case Studies", where they read about a company facing a specific situation. The students then analyze the case and come up with a solution. Hence, the more case studies that they read, the more familiar they will be in the real world when they face business situations.

This concept of taking reps and being exposed to a large number of situations is what separates elite performers. Think about the difference between the top quarterbacks with their peers. Every NFL quarterback has certain physical attributes. Being of a certain size and having a strong arm is needed in order to be drafted.

The way that these 3 quarterbacks are able to achieve success is through their minds. Its their ability to read defenses, understand the situation, and to make the right decision. The ability to do this comes from seeing the situation numerous times. They know what the defense is doing based on seeing it before. It's the same concept of when a person studies for a test, and finds the practice question on the actual exam.

For example, Tom Brady reported goes over the gameplan with head coach Bill Belichick numerous times a week, and also goes over every possible play that may be used in a game.

"He meets with Belichick three times a week to talk over the gameplan -- every coverage, every hot read, every play," states Bishop in Sports Illustrated. "He summons his backups an hour before the Saturday team meetings and goes over the entire call sheet, typically between 100 and 110 plays. Twice. He asks the QBs to arrive an hour early on gameday, too, then goes over everything again. Twice."

For these quarterbacks, the rise of modern technology has greatly helped them prepare and study. The ability to have the opponent's defenses, game film, and their own playbook on a tablet has been a great invention for quarterbacks who love to study.

Dan Hanzus wrote on NFL.com that Peyton Manning is hardly ever seen without an iPad.

"The iPad is ubiquitous," Hanzus writes. "I talked to several of Manning's Denver Broncos teammates during Super Bowl Media Day, and the iPad kept coming up."

Former Broncos tight end Julius Thomas told Hanzus that Manning "never sets it down. He's got it in the training room, he's got it in the lunchroom. He never stops preparing."

A viral picture of Peyton Manning emerged at the end of 2013 that shows how dedicated he is to getting his reps. According to the explanation given by the Denver Broncos, Manning was forced to sit out of a practice due to an injury to his right ankle. Not wanting to waste anytime, Manning found a way to treat his ankle yet still get his reps.

The picture shows Manning sitting next to a cold tub with his right ankle soaking in the tub. While sitting on a chair next to the tub, Manning is holding an iPad and watching game tape. So far, this seems to be normal behavior, as many people have sat soaking their feet while holding reading materials. But the way that Peyton Manning takes it to another level is that he was also wearing his football helmet. He was listening to the Offensive Coordinator call plays from practice that was taking place on the practice field. He was also repeating the play calls to another teammate who was also forced to sit out of practice due to injury. He wanted to follow along, and to keep getting his reps. All while treating his injured ankle in a cold tub and watching game tape on his iPad.

As Deadspin wrote about the picture, "Peyton Manning is more dedicated to football than you will ever be to anything in your life."

Peyton Manning was doing all of this after he already won a Super Bowl and numerous MVP awards. But that is why he is one of the best quarterback ever. He is always looking to learn and to get his mental reps.

2. Evaluation

Although players watch a lot of film, the way they are watching the games is very different from how fans watch the game. They aren't watching the games with their buddies and drinking beer and eating chicken wings. They are watching the games closely to see what they are doing wrong, or finding tiny advantages that they can exploit.

During his 2014 MVP season, Aaron Rodgers threw 520 passes. He had 5 interceptions. Four of his interceptions occurred after the ball deflected off of the intended receiver's hands. Thus, according to MMQB's Peter King, Aaron Rodgers only threw 1 interception all year due to a poor decision.

Rodgers went over in detail as to how that play developed, and how he ended up making the poor decision. He breaks down where he made the errors, and how his decision making process failed him on that play. He critically analyzed his own performance, and found the errors that he made. By studying the play closely, Rodgers was able to learn from the experience and find ways to minimize errors in the future.

Closely examining interceptions is something that the Packers organization emphasizes. According to former NFL quarterback Rich Gannon, "I've been doing the Packers' preseason games for 10 years," he tells King. "And I can tell you that when their quarterbacks throw interceptions, every one of them is gone over so thoroughly it's like a crime scene investigation."

Looking over each play so closely like a crime scene investigation is something that Peyton Manning does each offseason. Les Carpenter of Yahoo Sports wrote about how meticulous Peyton Manning was after each season while he was with the Indianapolis Colts.

Starting on the first Monday of March, Peyton Manning would arrive at the Colts facility at 6:30 am and lock himself in a room with the Offensive Coordinator and Quarterbacks Coach. The three men would sit down, turn on a television screen, and watch the first offensive play of the previous season.

Carpenter writes that the men would break down the play to its barest bones, and study every aspect of it. "Did they play work? If not, why? Was it blocked right? Were the receivers in the best position? How about the running back? Did it turn into a sack? Manning HATED sacks. What could they do to prevent sacks?"

They would write down all of their thoughts about the play, constantly thinking about how they could do things better. After analyzing the play thoroughly, the three men moved on to the second play of the season.

They then proceed to do that for every single offensive play that was run the previous season. To give an example of how many plays they were looking at, in 2009, when the Colts made it to the Super Bowl, they had 980 offensive plays that year. Manning and his coaches would go over each play and report back to the room at 6:30 the next day until they went through the entire season.

That is what elite performers do when they are studying. Watching film or reading case studies is not a passive activity. They are constantly thinking about how the situation unfolded, what decisions were made, and whether those decisions were successful. They are actively involved in the situation, and trying to get better.

Confidence

The payoff for studying is clearly shown on the field during games. The first payoff is that it gives the quarterback a high level of confidence knowing that they are prepared for everything that the defense might throw at them.

As Aaron Rodgers told the Milwaukee-Wisconsin Journal Sentinel, his deep analysis of past mistakes gives him the confidence to go out and make good plays.

"I try to focus on the positive things, but I can learn, personally, better from my mistakes than my good plays," he tells Lori Nickel. "I mean, I expect to play well. I don't think that's cockiness, I just think I prepare to play well every week. I put in the time, I watch film, I study, I practice, I talk to the receivers, the tight ends, the running backs. We get on the same page."

"So when I get in the game, I expect to play well."

This preparation allows Rodgers to exploit any mistakes made by his opponent. In the opening weeks of the 2015 season, Rodgers used his mastery of situations to take advantages of confusion between plays. As Rob Demovsky of ESPN wrote after a Monday

Night Football game against the Kansas City Chiefs, "Not only is Rodgers the best quarterback in the NFL, he's also the smartest. He's quick to recognize when teams want to sub for matchups or rest, and he's perhaps the best at making them pay for being overzealous. He caught the Chiefs with 12 men on the field twice in the first half of Monday night's 38-28 win. Both were on third-and-1 situations."

Once he's able to get the defense to commit a penalty, Rodgers goes for the jugular. Due to the rules of the NFL, when a defense commits a penalty, play continues as normal. If the offense is able to complete a big play, they have the option of keeping the big play. If they miss on the play, then they can accept the penalty committed by the defense and get the yards. In essence, the offense has a free play.

According to ESPN, Rodgers knows how to exploit these situations to his team's advantage. In four free plays against the Chiefs, Rodgers averaged 25.5 yards in passing which included a touchdown and a 52 yard pass.

In the first two games of the season, Rodgers used these situations on numerous occasions. He threw a 34 yard pass in the season opener against Chicago on a free play. Against the Seattle Seahawks in Week 2, Rodgers got the defense to jump offsides on three occasions, and threw a 22 yard completion, a 52 yard completion, and a 29 yard touchdown on those free plays.

As Demovsky writes, "It's like playing with house money for Rodgers. He knows he has a free 5 yards in his pocket and has nothing to lose."

Another great example of seeing how preparation can impact a game in real time was when Peyton Manning and the Colts faced the New York Jets for a trip to the Super Bowl in January 2010. At one point in the first half, the Colts were down 17-6 before Manning lead them to a touchdown with about a minute left in the half.

Down 17-13 entering the second half, all of the preparation, studying, and practice Manning goes through before a game paid off. Peyton was able to figure out the NFL's number 1 defense and score 17 unanswered points as the Colts beat the Jets 30-17 and earned a trip to the Super Bowl.

Hank Gola of the New York Daily News explained that it was very clear the film study paid off for Manning.

"Very early on, it looked as though the Jets had Peyton Manning confused. As it turned out, he was just feeling them out," Gola wrote. "Once he figured out the Jets' basic approach, Manning was able to exploit several mismatches to his advantage. Once the Colts solved the Jets' blitz schemes, he was shooting fish in a barrel."

Manning told the press that to prepare for the game in January 2010, he went back into the film archives to study a 2005 Colts-Ravens game, when the head coach of the Jets was the defensive coordinator for the Baltimore Ravens. "I studied the 2005 Colts-Ravens game and I said I think they might play this defense," Manning was quoted by Gola. "That's kind of what they did today. He has his style of defense and he goes back to things."

By studying a 5 year old game, Peyton Manning was able to outsmart the number one defense for a trip to the Super Bowl. In fact, former teammate Ryan Diem told the press that Peyton Manning KNEW he had the Jets' defense figured out.

"Ryan Diem caught the smirk," writes Vic Carucci for NFL.com. "A few times while waiting for the Indianapolis Colts to run their next play, the veteran offensive tackle noticed that Peyton Manning was actually smirking in the direction of the top-ranked defense in the NFL. That was when Diem knew that his quarterback had pretty much solved the puzzle that is Rex Ryan's blitz-happy, multiple-look scheme."

Carucci continues, "Think you're going to fool the lanky general in the blue and white uniform and shoulder pads with some elaborate strategy that he hasn't seen, something he wouldn't be prepared to handle?"

"Guess again."

Review Questions

1. How much time and effort are you putting into your work? Not just the actual working part, but in the preparation aspect of your job. Elite performers all put in additional time honing their craft. All three quarterbacks do more than what is asked by their coaches. They all develop additional training programs on their own to get better. Are you doing the same? Are you learning new skills on your own time? Are you trying to improve some aspect of your performance at night when you have time?

2. Are you getting as much reps as possible? Whatever your field, having more experience and opportunities to learn will benefit you. Seeing things in action, talking to other professionals, and getting as much exposure to the environment will help improve your performance. Great quarterbacks watch film all the time to familiarize themselves to defensive coverages and to find out where the holes are. The more material you study, the more effective you will be.

3. But it's not simply a matter of being exposed to new material. You have to actively think about the materials you are reading. Peyton Manning goes over every single play from the previous season, asking himself what worked, what didn't work. You have to attack your own work in the same manner. After each sales call, ask yourself what worked. After each presentation, review the video of it and see where your message wasn't as strong. After each game, look closely at your individual performance to see where you fell short.

Practice

A belief that all three elite quarterbacks share is the value that they place on practice. To them, practice isn't something simply to go through. When players are growing up, the concept of practice may not be that fun. Practice is when players have to go through drills, run sprints, and do the same play over and over. Games are where the action is. That's when the players friends and family can come out and see them play. But in order to play in NFL games on Sundays, work and effort must be put in during practice. And all three quarterbacks fully understand that.

"Marvin Harrison always had a great quote," Peyton Manning told Mike Chappell of the Indy Star. "He said they pay you to practice, the games you play for free. I always thought that was a great quote because it's easy to play the games. Everybody can get excited to play the games. But are you willing to pay the price and sacrifice in the months of March through September?"

Practice Like Your Job Depends on It. Because It Does.

Former Bronco Rahim Moore talked to Benjamin Hochman of the Denver Post about Peyton Manning's attitude towards practice. Moore stated that Manning behaves in practice as if he's one bad move away from being cut. "We know when he gets on the field, he's going hard - like as if he never had a penny," Moore is quoted as saying. "That's how hard he works. You would think he never had done a commercial, none of that. He's training like he's a free agent."

"Let it sink in," writes Hochman. "What a quote, right? Peyton Manning, one of the best talents of his generation, attacks practice as if his career is on the line, as if one bad day at the office and he's coaching high school, telling stories about once going to an NFL camp with Peyton Manning."

Peyton Manning treats practice like his job depends on it, because it actually does. In a league based on results, if Manning is no longer able to win on Sundays, than he will quickly find himself removed in favor of a younger, stronger quarterback. The only way to keep his job is to keep winning, and he can't do that without putting in the effort at practice.

"I had a coach taught me at an early age of treating practice like a game," Manning told Hochman. "To me this is where you become a better football team out here on the practice field. You don't just show up on a game and expect to be a good football team."

When told that teammates stated that Manning practiced as if his next contract depended on it, Manning said that "I think somebody taught me to practice like that at a young age. That would be my advice to any young players. Like I said, taking care of each other, you don't want to injure any player out there on the field because you're competing out here, you are going full speed up until maybe that point of contact. Trying to put yourself in those precious situations so when you get to the game, you feel like you've been there before."

This concept of making practice as similar to a game is something that Tom Brady also preaches. Former Patriots defensive lineman Vince Wilfork stated that the offense and defense at practice would become very competitive with each other in order to create a game environment.

"He always comes to work and trust me, we trash talk a lot in practice," Wilfork told local media station WEEI. "I'm in his ear and he's in my ear, but at the same time we make practice live and we make practice competitive because we try to get it as close to a game [atmosphere] as possible."

Brady himself views practice as part of the competition towards the other team. Practice and the game are the same things in his mind.

The Patriots can't beat a team on Sunday if they didn't already beat them during the week by practicing harder.

During the playoffs in January 2015, Brady stated that as soon as the opponent is determined, then the game actually starts.

"You watch the Denver game and Indy play, and as soon as that game ends it's like, "Boom!" and the clock starts. It's a race to see who can prepare the best over the course of the week."

To Brady, competing with other teams doesn't just take place during the 60 minutes of game time. The week leading up to the game is part of the competition as well. He doesn't limit his idea of competition to the game on Sunday, but rather the entire week leading up to the game as well. Brady is going to want to practice and prepare harder as part of the competition against the opponent. The game on Sunday is simply the last part of that competition.

Practice Is A Time To Make Mistakes

How elite quarterbacks use their practice time is also important to note. They don't just go through the motions and use it to stay active. Rather, there are key goals that they strive for during practice to help them improve their game.

In the same way that they watch film closely to correct their mistakes and find advantages, these quarterbacks actively look for ways to find mistakes in order to get better.

Former Broncos cornerback Tracy Porter told a story to Ryan McGee of ESPN about how he picked off a pass made by Manning in practice. However, a couple of plays later, Manning was able to burn Porter with a deep pass.

After practice ended, Porter was walking back to the locker room when he felt a hand on his shoulder. Manning was going out of his way to stop Porter to talk about the interception, as well as how Peyton was able to burn him deep.

"You tell me what I did wrong on that first play and I'll tell you what you did wrong on that next play," Manning told Porter. "That's the only way we're going to get better. Deal?"

McGee writes that this incident left a lasting impression on the cornerback. "Months later, Porter still shakes his head while telling the story. 'Dang right, that was a deal," he says. "He wants me to be better so he can be better. And he wants to be better to help me get better. I'll follow a man like that into any game, anywhere, any way."

Aaron Rodgers also uses practice to achieve specific goals. During practice, Rodgers purposely throws passes where the ball may be at a higher risk for an interception. He told the media that during practice he tries to put the ball into places where both the receiver and the defender has a chance to get the ball. That way, Rodgers is able to see what the receiver is capable of doing.

"You have to show it in practice in order for me to feel comfortable making those throws in the game," Rodgers told ESPN. "That's kind of what this is all about. You make some of these throws and see how guys respond."

Rodgers doesn't just strive to be perfect in practice. He understands that practice is the time to be trying out new things. Making mistakes during practice is fine as long as there is a purpose behind the action. Rodgers is actively trying to see how his receivers fight for jump balls. He is able to use this knowledge during games to see how which receivers would be able to beat tight coverage. If this leads to mistakes and interceptions during practice, so be it.

Use Your Practice Time Wisely

For both Tom Brady and Aaron Rodgers, practice time is important to them due to the way their careers started. For both future Hall-of-Fame quarterbacks, their careers initially started as the 2nd string quarterbacks. During their first season in the NFL, both Tom Brady and Aaron Rodgers only got to throw a football during practice.

To this day, Tom Brady refuses to let his backups get any of his reps during practice. In addition to the benefit of getting as much situational game experience, he doesn't want to give the backups any chance of taking his job. "That's how I got my job," Brady told former backups Matt Cassel and Brian Hoyer.

Perhaps the best use of practice time in the history of the NFL was done by Aaron Rodgers. He is widely considered to be the best quarterback in the NFL during the 2015 season. It can easily be argued that he was the best quarterback in the league in 2014, when he won the MVP. He has won a Super Bowl ring, and is a shoe-in for the Hall of Fame.

But it's worth remembering that for his first 3 years in the NFL, the only football that Aaron Rodgers played was during practice, as he was the backup to Brett Favre.

As Greg Bishop wrote in the New York Times, "In his rookie season, in 2005, Aaron Rodgers almost never played on Sundays. Instead, he played on Wednesdays, Thursdays, Fridays and Saturdays, in practice, against increasingly agitated teammates."

The main role of a backup quarterback on an NFL team is to be the scout team quarterback. The scout team runs the plays that the opponent will probably run during the game, giving the defense a chance to prepare.

"The plays for the scout team, run by Rodgers, were supposed to be scripted, the tempo purposely slow," Bishop writes. "Instead, Rodgers tossed deep passes and no-look passes and tight spirals," frustrating the starting defense. "By Week 11 of his rookie year, Rodgers said an assistant coach notified him that "the head man doesn't appreciate all the Saturday no-look passes because you're making the defense look bad." He added, "He wants you to knock it off a little bit."

So what does Aaron Rodgers do? He starts to choreograph touchdown dances with his fellow scout team members. Former cornerback Al Harris told Bishop that Rodgers "would do the championship belt dance. He would spike the ball. He was a trip."

Even after getting the starting job and winning a Super Bowl, Rodgers continues to push the defense at practice. "Look, Aaron still enjoys practice," said Packers General Manager Ted Thompson. "He still wants to get on the defense's nerves, rattle guys. That's just him."

In addition to frustrating the first string defense, Rodgers made sure that he wasn't just moping on the bench. Instead of being frustrated that he wasn't playing and demanding to be traded, Rodgers made sure that he was using the time to improve his skillset.

Current Green Bay Packers head coach Mike McCarthy arrived during Rodgers second season. McCarthy immediately recognized the special talent he had in Rodgers, and started him on a special training program that he called his "Quarterback School."

McCarthy made Rodgers go through drills to improve his motor skills, his hand-eye coordination, finger dexterity and throwing mechanics. Rodgers worked so hard during practice and on his own that by the end of his second year, the Packers head coach and general manager viewed him as a "starter who happened not to start," according to the New York Times.

The coaching staff began making Rodgers do the tasks that most starting quarterbacks do. He studied every single play from the previous season. He took the first-string reps at spring practice when Brett Favre stayed home. Greg Bishop writes that in the offseason between Rodgers second and third season, Rodgers would spend 10 hours studying film and 3 hours on practicing on the field each week. He also spent time studying every pass Tom Brady made during the 2007 season.

Rodgers increased both his physical skills as well as his knowledge about the Packers playbook that he was able to think more deeply about the game, and to find ways to exploit opposing defenses.

"Eventually, Rodgers focused less on learning the Packers' offense and more on clarifying why defenses ran certain coverages, schemes or fronts. Now, when Rodgers drops back to pass, he does not look for his receivers. He looks for defenders, where they are, where they might move, what that means or could mean. Then he throws for receivers headed toward open space," writes Bishop.

Keep in mind that all of this work was done during practice. All of this work put in by Aaron Rodgers was when he was holding a clipboard for the starting quarterback during games. Not once did Rodgers publicly demand to be traded, or cause any problems within the organization. He instead used his time wisely. He used the time spent backing up a Hall-of-Famer by studying, by making mistakes away from the public glare, and working hard to improve his own performance.

General manager Ted Thompson said it best: "For three years, his time on the stage was in practice. He put it to good use."

Review Questions

1. Too often, we view practice as something to get through. We view practice as a grind that simply isn't as exciting as the games. There are no crowds, our friends and families can't see us perform, and it can get boring doing the same thing over and over.

However, elite performers find a way to stay engaged during practice. Tom Brady views the amount of work and preparation he puts into practice as part of the competition against that week's opponent. He wonders who can prepare the most between the two teams and simply lets his competitive nature take over. The end result, obviously, is that he gets better during the week and sees great results on game days.

How do you view your training time? Do you view it as a chore? Or do you approach it with intensity?

2. Are you taking risks during your practice or training sessions? Are you failing? If not, then you probably are growing or learning a new skill. The purpose of practice is to improve the skills you already have, and to learn new ones. You can't learn new skills without making any mistakes. Aaron Rodgers throws numerous interceptions during practice because he wants to see what the receiver's can do. Practice is the time to do that.

If you are dominating your drills and not making any mistakes during practice, then it might be a good idea to start changing things up.

Mindset

Aaron Rodgers, Tom Brady, and Peyton Manning have succeeded in one of the most competitive industries in the world. There can only be 32 starting NFL quarterbacks each year, and their performance is closely examined by opposing teams, the media, and the general public. Any flaws or gaps in their skillset is easily noticed and widely shared.

Despite the incredible pressure and criticism that they face, they have been able to constantly perform on the biggest stage. In this section, we analyze how they are able to continually motivate themselves to work hard, and how they are able to fight through and achieve their goals.

Setbacks Don't Ruin Their Self-Esteem

As previously mentioned, Aaron Rodgers and Tom Brady both spent their first year in the league as backup quarterbacks. The slights and setbacks faced by both quarterbacks throughout their entire football life have been pretty big. The fact that both men were able to use those setbacks as motivation says a lot about their mindset.

While at the University of Michigan, Tom Brady wasn't even considered to be the best quarterback on the team. He wasn't named the starting quarterback until his senior year, and even then he faced competition. During the first couple of games during that season, Brady was sharing reps with Drew Henson, who was widely considered to be a stronger quarterback. It wasn't until several games into the season that Brady was named the full-time quarterback.

While at Michigan, Brady took the time to get help from the university staff and learned how to use the adversity to his advantage. Seth Wickersham writes that Brady eventually realized that these trials and tribulations helped him become the man that he is.

"Brady walked into the office of Greg Harden, the director of athletic counseling at Michigan, and said, "I need help." Brady spent Friday nights before games in Harden's office, learning to control the anger he felt about being a back up, then splitting time with Drew Henson. He graduated with an unbreakable self-belief," writes Wickersham. "And one day this winter, during a round of golf, Brady told his dad, 'I couldn't be where I am now without experiencing those things.'"

Due to his lack of playing time in college and a lack of impressive physical features, NFL scouts and general managers didn't think Tom Brady was an NFL caliber quarterback. In the 2000 NFL draft, Tom Brady wasn't selected until the 199th pick. 6 quarterbacks were selected by other teams before Tom Brady.

Although Aaron Rodgers was selected in the first round, he too faced numerous adversities in his career. While a senior in high school, Rodgers had dreams of playing college ball at Florida State. "But Florida State didn't want Rodgers," says Jeremy Schaap on E:60. "Nor did any other Division 1 school."

With no offers for a college scholarship, Rodgers enrolled at Butte Community College, where he played football for one season. While there, the head coach of the University of California came to scout a wide receiver on Butte's team. That was when Rodgers was discovered and given a scholarship to Cal.

After two seasons at Cal, Rodgers decides to enter the NFL draft. In that draft, the top two quarterback prospects were Aaron Rodgers and Alex Smith from Utah. As is customary, both quarterbacks were invited to the draft so that when their names were called, they could walk out on stage with the jersey of their new team.

The San Francisco 49ers selected Alex Smith with the number 1 pick. Rodgers, waiting in the green room, wasn't selected second. He also wasn't selected in the top 10. He wasn't even selected in the top 20 picks. He was eventually selected by the Green Bay Packers with the 24th overall pick.

As team after team kept passing on him, Rodgers was forced to sit in the green room. The story of the draft suddenly became about Rodgers dropping in the draft, as television cameras continued to show him backstage waiting for his name to be called.

According to Sports Illustrated, Rodgers was sitting in the green room for four hours and 18 minutes between the time Alex Smith was drafted and when his own name was called.

"It's embarrassing," Rodgers told E;60. "You know the whole world's watching. Your phone's buzzing every two minutes, and you hope it's a team calling. But it's just your buddy's saying 'Hey, nice hair, nice suit. Smile a little bit. Kiss your Mom', just making jokes. But it's hard to laugh in a situation when you know everyone is laughing at you."

After sitting behind Brett Favre for three seasons, Favre retired in the offseason before the 2008 season. However, before the season started, Favre changed his mind and "all but demanded that he get his starting job back", according to Schaap. Many fans in Green Bay still had strong feelings for Favre, with chants of "Bring Back Favre" taking place during training camp.

Despite all of this, Rodgers didn't let it affect his own self belief. He didn't allow the external circumstances to affect his confidence in his ability to play quarterback in the NFL.

Both Brady and Rodgers used the adversity to their advantage. They used it to fuel their motivation to get better, to improve on their own skills, and to work harder to prove others wrong.

Think about how they could have allowed these issues to affect them if they didn't have a strong self image. They both could have listened the experts and believe that they weren't good enough to a successful quarterback. Aaron Rodgers could have given up on football after high school when Division 1 schools didn't give him a scholarship. Tom Brady could have believed the NFL scouts and GM's when he was the 6th quarterback selected in the 2000 draft, and simply accept that he will never be a great quarterback.

When people are being judged and evaluated by others, it is so easy to allow the opinions of others to impact them. Whether it's athletes, job candidates, even students, it is very easy to allow the judgements of others to become ingrained into the performer's mind. If everyone says I'm bad at this, than I must be bad at this.

The special skill and mindset that Tom Brady and Aaron Rodgers showed is that they never allowed the judgement of others to impact them. Just because professional scouts and football executives didn't think they were any good didn't stop them from working hard. They stayed true to who they believed they were.

But how did they exactly do that? It's one thing to say, "Stay positive", or "Believe in Yourself". But that doesn't give the person a roadmap or blueprint on how to do that. It appears as if the following two traits have helped these quarterbacks achieve success and the right mindset to work hard.

1. Competitiveness

As previously mentioned, Aaron Rodgers and Tom Brady used setbacks and critical judgements against them as motivation. Rather than letting the opinions of others bring them down, they used it as fuel to work harder. They wanted to prove that they were capable of being successful NFL quarterbacks, and that's a type of competitiveness that is needed to succeed in any industry.

"He is so competitive," Vince Wilfork said of Brady. "That's the first thing I always see. And everybody always asks me, 'How is Tom?' I don't think there's anybody else in this locker room that is more competitive than Tom."

The desire to compete with the best is a desire that must come from within the person. Aaron Rodgers and Tom Brady aren't motivated by a desire for money or awards. Rather, they are striving to be the best they can be, and to be the best at their positions.

According to Dr. Kevin Burke, a sports psychology professor, having a competitive desire to be the best can prove to be a long-lasting motivation, as opposed to a desire to get a huge contract.

"Athletes motivated by an internal desire to succeed and be the best at what they do tend to stay in their sport longer and are more satisfied with their experiences," Dr. Burke writes in The Sporting News. "There are cases when athletes who end up with many rewards, particularly a high-paying contract, may lose some of their internal motivation to succeed. Usually this can be seen by a decrease in their performance and even a complacency on the court or field."

Aaron Rodgers uses the slights against him to stay motivated. Despite winning MVP trophies and a Super Bowl ring, Rodgers is still able to keep a competitive mindset to perform at a high level. It's sort of a two-way street. The adversity he faced allows him to stay motivated to keep performing, while his motivation to keep performing allowed him to work through the adversity.

"In Aaron Rodger's case, he uses the fact that he was drafted later than expected as a constant reminder to work hard to show others the mistake they made by not drafting him. The MVP awards, Super Bowl appearances and lucrative contract only serve to enhance his motivation to succeed," writes Dr. Burke.

2. Be in the Moment

Another way that Tom Brady is able to control his mindset is to simply be in the moment. He actively tries to stay present in the moment. He doesn't allow distractions or past mistakes to continue to haunt him. Rather, he simply focuses on the task at hand and strives to give his best at that exact moment.

"When I'm playing football, I appreciate it. I'm nowhere else. I'm in the present," Brady told Michael Strahan in an interview on Fox. "That's probably the best part of my life. You talk about how you enjoy life, how you find balance. It's to live in the present. To live like a kid. Why do kids have so much fun? It's because they just care about what they're doing. You do that when you're on the football field. It's probably the only place where I can truly do that, where I truly am my authentic self."

To Brady, it comes down to what he is able to control. He can't control how people compare him to Joe Montana or Peyton Manning. He can't control the types of wide receivers the Patriots have on their team. All his can do is control his work ethic, his effort, and his own expectations of himself.

Seth Wickersham of ESPN highlighted how Brady focuses on the moment to ensure his success. "A few months ago, Brady watched Jiro Dreams of Sushi, a documentary about an 85-year old who loves to cook and wakes up each day trying to improve at doing so. "It smacked me in the face as a reaffirmation," Brady says. "Just be in the moment. What's better than what you're doing? Nothing." He knows, as his dad says, that as soon as Belichick gets "a quarterback who is better for a dollar less, he'll be gone." He won't allow himself to be outwork or overpriced. He won't allow himself to feel doubt. He will always test the limits of what he can control, because it's the only way of controlling what he loves to do."

In a highly competitive league, Brady fully understands and accepts the fact that things will be out of his control. If it wasn't for an insane catch by David Tyree of the Giants in the 2008 Super Bowl, then Brady would have one more Super Bowl ring and a perfect season under his belt.

But Brady, Manning, and Rodgers all realize that they can't win every year. They all put in the work to be prepared as best they can, but don't let tough losses continue to haunt them. They all live in the present on focus solely on what they can do at that moment to be a better quarterback.

That sentiment was shared with Brady by another Super Bowl winning quarterback. After Tom Brady and the Patriots lost in the playoffs to the Baltimore Ravens in 2012, Brady received a text from Kurt Warner:

Being the best doesn't mean you always win. It just means you win more than anybody else.

Review Questions:

1. How strong is your self belief in your talents and abilities? If you receive one negative evaluation, will you begin to question all of your skills?

Imagine if the experts in whatever field you are in determined that you weren't in the top tier. Imagine if your boss or coach thought that you weren't the best at your position. Maybe this has already happened and you have been rejected for a team or denied a promotion. How are you responding to the setback? Have you subconsciously begun to think that the people who rejected you must know what they are doing?

Tom Brady and Aaron Rodgers never the judgements of others affect their own confidence and self-belief. Rather than accepting those negative judgements, the two MVP quarterbacks instead decided to prove them wrong. They didn't wallow in pity, blame others, or believe that they had limited potential. Instead, they decided to work really hard.

2. How focused are you in the present? Are you letting past mistakes or failure continue to haunt you? Are you allowing the opinions of others to dictate how you perform? In today's world, there is nothing you can do to prevent others from making comments about something. From social media to YouTube comments, there is nothing you can do to keep people from commenting on your performance. What you can control, however, is your response to them.

When Aaron Rodgers took over for Brett Favre, he didn't let the chants of "Bring Back Favre" distract him from putting in the work or studying film. Peyton Manning didn't let a neck surgery and questions about his age stop him from coming back and leading his team to the Super Bowl. Tom Brady didn't let questions about deflated football distract him from leading his team to a Super Bowl victory. They were able to do these things because the simply focused on what they had to do at that moment.

Keys to Success

1. It takes a lot of work to be the best. You have to find ways to create additional training programs for yourself outside of your normal schedule if you want to be at the top of your field.

2. Get as much repetitions in your field as possible. Whether it's reading case studies or performing as much as possible, the more familiar you are with your industry, the more you will succeed.

3. Evaluate your past actions closely. Look at everything that you have done and closely examine what worked, what didn't work, and what needs to change.

4. Use your practice or training time wisely. Don't do the same drills or exercises all the time. If you aren't making mistakes at practice, then you need to change it up.

5. In order to beat your opponent at the game, you have to first beat them at practice. You do that by working harder and preparing better.

6. If you lack confidence, it can be gained when you know you are prepared.

7. Never let other people's opinion or evaluations become how you think about your own performance.

8. Allow your internal goals to be a better performer guide you. Don't get so focused on external goals such as awards and money.

9. Stay focused on the present in order to forget past mistakes and to eliminate distractions.

10. You are in control of your own effort, your own work ethic, and the amount of time you put into preparation.

Additional Leadership Case Studies

The Strategy Concepts of Bill Belichick

The Management Ideas of Nick Saban

The Motivational Techniques of Urban Meyer

The Turnaround Strategies of Jim Harbaugh

The Leadership Lessons of Gregg Popovich

The Team Building Strategy of Steve Kerr

About Leadership Case Studies

Leadership Case Studies provides brief reports and analysis on successful individuals. We focus on the habits, strategies, and mindsets of high-performing people in the sports, business, and entertainment industries.

Started in July 2015, Leadership Case Studies released its first case study on University of Alabama Football Coach Nick Saban, winner of 4 national championships.

Website:
http://www.leadershipcasestudies.com

Made in the USA
Las Vegas, NV
28 January 2021